SECRETS OF THE MANY WELLS

Lora Brand

COPYRIGHTS

Copyrights
©Lora Brand [2025]
All Rights reserved
No portion of this book may be reproduced, distributed or transmitted, in any form or by any means, including photocopying, recording or any other electronic methods, without written permission from the publisher or author, except in the case of brief quotations and certain other non-commercial uses permitted by copywrite law.

The advice and strategies contained in this publication may not be suitable for your situation. You should consult with a professional when appropriate. Neither the publisher nor the author shall be liable for any loss of profit or any other commercial damages, including but not limited to special, incidental, consequential, personal, or any other damages.

National Library of Australia cataloguing-in-Publication entry
Author: Brand, Lora, Author.

Editor: van der Merwe, Nadia, Editor

Title: Secrets of the Many Wells

[2] Heart and Soul Series [Lora Brand]

ISBN: 9781763786431

Book Cover by [Lora Brand]

Poetry (Lora Brand 2025)

Christian Life Anecdotes

Table of Contents

Copyrights 1
Author's note 5
Acknowledgements 7
    Wells of sustenance Poem 8
Introduction 9
    Thirst Poem 11
Wells 13
    Wells Poem 17
The well of addiction 19
    Addiction Poem 25
The well of love and relationships 27
    Love and relationship Poem 33
The well of depression, suicide and self-harm ... 34
    Depression, suicide and self-harm Poem 38
    Unforgiveness Poem 44
The well of the past 45
    The past Poem 51
The well of pain 52
    Pain Poem 57
The well of wealth 59
    Wealth Poem 62
The well of escape 63
    Escape Poem 66
The well of Living Waters 67

Living Waters Poem 79
Conclusion 80

Author's Note

The purpose of this book is to assist readers to understand and recognise a thirst that we are all born with, a thirst to be happy, secure, fulfilled and satisfied.

We are born to be in relationships, not to be alone.

Regardless of how one believes we arrived, relationships are the key to a healthy life. We are not meant to be alone or self-sufficient. We are at our best when we work together. We build each other up. We encourage one another. This is healthy living.

Unfortunately, relationships hurt, living can hurt. How do we maintain a healthy life?

I believe that it stems from the wells that we drink from.

Not all wells are helpful, not all wells will quench our thirst.

Throughout this book, the poetry depicts the many wells we may knowingly or unknowingly drink from. Initially, chapters describe destructive types of wells, revealing the effect it may have on the soul, then I share about the Well of Living Waters I've found to nourish all areas of my life. It is my hope that this book may help you, the reader, discern which wells you drink from, and which wells you may need to let run dry.

To have the courage to change the watering holes where necessary is difficult. We may need help to purposefully choose wells that are of benefit, bringing, peace, joy, patience, nourishment, and so on, to our innermost-being. Life offers many beneficial wells, that we could draw from and embrace the refreshing and serenity they bring to our soul. Many times, in my life I have drawn and continue to draw from these wells; they have been the solidarity in my very existence and purpose, as well as pivotal moments in moving me to bring necessary changes in my life.

I believe we all could change our lives for the better, once we recognise areas that need change.

Acknowledgements

Many thanks to the community, where I live. I have had the pleasure of being a volunteer in various organisations. I have made many valuable friends and connections.

I have had the privilege of working as a volunteer in my community in the areas of homelessness, addictions, mental health and church groups. Thank you to Mackay Christian Family for allowing me to lead in various forms. Thank you to Selectability Mackay for mentoring me as a volunteer.

I am truly thankful for all those that have touched my heart in the community: those who have inspired me to flourish, those who have walked alongside me, through my life's journey. I thank you all.

For those that have become my closest friends and have challenged me where needed, I appreciate your honesty and friendship.

Thank you to my friend, Sharon, who takes the time to proofread my work, and isn't afraid to be honest.

Thank you to my editor, Nadia, for your kindness and patience in helping make the dream a reality.

And my utmost thanks to Jesus who led me to the Well which quenches my thirst daily.

WELLS OF SUSTENANCE POEM

My heart is rich in value, just as silver and gold,
Sitting by the beach, majestic, beauty to behold.
Drinking in all its beauty, drawn to offload thought,
The serenity and peace cannot be sold or bought.

Surrounded by great friends, encouraging me day by day,
Standing with me in all seasons, no words could ever say.
Knowing they are there, to call on when I need,
Keeping me in balance, to see that I succeed.

Sport, another avenue to refresh my inner-being,
Endorphins, dopamine overload, time and time again.
Long brisk walks, meandering, through from tree to tree,
Rejuvenating feelings of joy relaxed and carefree.

Spending time with family, who know my thoughts and fears,
Who hold me up when blue and wipe away my tears.
That unconditional love, no comparison to another,
The blessings and the joy, of a sister or a brother.

The world is as a diamond, glistening at me,
Various facets showing off, for curious eyes to see.
Join a club, a group, a choir, the list becomes endless,
No need to stay and brood, when life becomes a mess.

This walk called life, at times not easy, depending on the season,
Causing me to search, for a purpose and a reason.
To be fulfilled and satisfied, a heart driven to feel whole,
At last, to find those wells, to quench my thirsty soul.

Introduction

Most of my life I have lived and breathed amongst people from all walks of life. I thrive from the joy of living amongst and alongside others. Through my own life's experiences, as well as theirs, I have learned the many forms of wells one may drink from.

The common thread I have learned through all affiliations as a volunteer, is that people desire relationships, friendships, purpose, security, love and self-worth.

I have sought out secrets to live life and be satisfied through drinking from wells that are good, healthy and helpful. I have learned that I can choose the wells to draw water from, water that nourishes my soul, the infilling and indwelling of peace, security, satisfaction and more.

Though it may not be easy to switch wells, it is not impossible.

Life can have moments that come with disappointments, heartache, loss, betrayal, joy, excitement, highs and lows. How we live life and navigate successfully is often determined by our wellsprings. Over the course of my life, I have quenched my thirst through various watering holes that I drank from.

The season I was in, or the emotions in my heart, would at times dictate how I would try to quench my unquenchable thirst, whether it be drinking from a well of despair, betrayal, fear, love or peace. This would determine some of my choices and actions. Not all choices I made were helpful or good for the soul, nevertheless life is a journey, a road to navigate.

Throughout my life of learning and mistakes, I hope to uncover some of the many wells from which one can drink from. What feeds the soul? Does it quench the heart, or does it cause an insatiable thirst?

I hope this book helps you uncover the many sources of wells that one may drink from as you journey through life.

Thirst Poem

A thirst so deep, it's difficult to explain,
The quest to satisfy is yet to remain.
How do I fill this desire in my soul,
Where do I go to fill the void, the hole?

Is it in the heavens, is it on this earth,
This deep hidden desire, thirsty since birth.
Where is this well, so I thirst no more,
Is it high on a mountain, is it behind a closed door?

Can I make it happen, or make it appear,
Will it fill this gap and hide my fear?
Do I simply earn this by being good,
Do I look to a statue carved in wood?

Is it in a building with friends all around,
Or in the air where gardens and trees surround?
Maybe it's in a chemical, or a liquid to drink,
Or quenched through a lover, what do you think?

Parched and thirsty, craving for more,
Which well knocks on your heart's door?
Oh, to be alone with sorrow and fears,
Which well will soothe all those tears?

The choices are endless, from many wells to draw,
Blinded at times, as issues lie deep in your core.
A heart may be wounded and scarred well within,
Causing poor choices, to drink from therein.

Which well do you drink from, is it good for your soul,
Will it lead to freedom, will it make you feel whole?
Will it bring you destruction, will it lead you to success,
Will it make you feel secure, or cause you to feel less?

Is it by the beach, stretching out for miles,
Causing one to hope with endless smiles.
Are the secrets of this well yet to find,
To drink from a source of a different kind?

Quenching one's thirst, till there is no more,
Amazingly refreshing the soul to restore.
This well is the key to rest and to peace,
Then, at last, the search may now cease.

Wells

All throughout history, and still today, wells were vital for people to survive. They were built to hold water, creating an endless source that can continually be drawn from. Communities thrived where there were wells and people didn't have to scatter to find water sources. The well provided a central source for all.

Wells were a very important part of life in biblical times. The water would sustain mankind, and was used for drinking, for watering flocks, fields and crops.

Wells were significant for gatherings of people. Women had their allotted times to draw water to supply their families. Travellers would come to quench their thirst and to water their livestock. Without wells, people perished.

A well often became a place of chatter, and often this would be the place young men would meet young women, and potentially life-long ties were formed. Discussions and friendships were made around a well.

I imagine women and how their chatter would encourage one another, counsel one another and lift each other up. I imagine burdens being shared and love being nurtured one to another. Imaginations of the young men gathered nearby, anticipating a wife with hopeful expectations – what a beautiful picture of community, help and health. Not only did they drink from the water but drew sustenance from one another. The wells were two-fold. They were a place to draw water and a place for teaching and learning. Going to the well must have been an exciting time for women, shepherds and young men. What a buzzing life source, full of activity.

Just as life and sustenance came from drawing from a well, death also may have come from it. The well may have carried stagnant or contaminated water. If the well was bad, then all who drank from it would have been affected with ill health or even death.

The life flow of people from a contaminated well would wither away. No life would flourish there, nor a city, nor a town that relies on that well. People would perish, and households would suffer from drinking from that contaminated well.

However, we do need to find wells to draw from, that will quench our inward thirst for acceptance, peace, love, relationships, and so on. It takes wisdom to discern good healthy wells, as opposed to stagnant, contaminated and poisonous wells.

We may not even be aware of which type of well we drink from to satisfy our thirsty souls.

Often in our society we take water for granted. We don't think about the source of where it comes from or if it is good water to drink. Then there are those who carefully choose their water source. They may research its quality and the value it has on their inner health. By choice they may purchase their water as opposed to drinking from the home supply in their taps. The financial cost is valued for the benefit of good inner health.

Choices we make can also come with a cost, whether financial or our own personal wellbeing. Just as it is a choice which water source we choose to drink from, it is also a choice which wellspring of life we drink from to satisfy our souls.

As you read through this book, we will uncover the secrets of many wells we drink from to quench the thirst within. The final chapter reveals a Well that I have found, one that continually refreshes and nourishes my soul.

Wells Poem

The well is a place to quench one's thirst,
A place in your heart where you run to first.
Could be a book or television, helping escape the mind,
Satisfying one's thoughts, keeping you blind.

Oh, to be thirsty and to seek out a well,
Not all are good, and some may compel.
Some will fill you for only a moment,
Some will cause pain and possible torment.

A well is the place to draw water for the soul,
Refreshing your innermost peace, where life may have stole.
To find that well is like discovering gold,
Forever sustaining you, from young to old.

Might be with close friends to help you sustain,
Stabilising your thoughts, helping you to remain.
Comforting your heart, inspiring you through,
Difficult circumstances that only you knew.

Might be those thoughts, locked in one's head,
Swirling round as you lie in your bed.
Daily consumed with much agitation,
Pre-occupied with feelings of loneliness and isolation.

Might be the anger of a hurt done wrong,
Playing over and over like a weary old song.
Leaving despair and destruction, stealing all joy,
Robbing one's life as a broken-down toy.

Many wells we drink from, the pick is yours,
Choose carefully, from those with open doors.
For not all will quench the innermost being,
Counterfeiting the truth, causing eyes not seeing.

Drink from those, that will sustain your life,
Keeping you at peace and out of strife.
Refreshing your mind, as you drink from their origin,
Calming your thoughts, the heart being still again.

The Well of Addiction

Addiction is not an emotion, nor is it simply a feeling. It is a deep longing or craving to take something, do something or feel something. Addiction takes hold in the brain, signalling pleasure and overriding the natural dopamine once the action is performed, or a substance has entered the body. It provides a 'fix' or high that only holds for a short while, then to leave us dissatisfied and empty again. Once addiction has taken root, various forms of symptoms are experienced by the addict during withdrawals, and the severity of the withdrawal process depends on the type of addiction.

Addiction can sneak up unsuspectingly. Unfortunately, many are tricked with a deception that it will never happen to them, a belief system that says, *I know what I am doing, and I am in control.*

At which point someone will become addicted to something varies from one person to another. Addiction is sly. Addiction is sneaky in the way it takes hold of our thoughts and lives. Addiction robs us of the freedom to simply say no.

Addiction begins with relationship. That substance, thing or action becomes trustworthy in what it can do for the addict. A relationship can be formed in that first instance. How does it make us feel? Does it give us a sense of freedom, boldness, happiness, escape from pain and stress? Unbeknownst to us, a trust relationship grows leading us to a deeper desire for more.

Much thought may not be given about that first encounter apart from some fun, a thrill or being *in* with the crowd. Once the ice is broken, it is much harder to say no and why would we? After all that experience was fun and seemingly harmless. A journey may begin with consuming alcohol or drug use more regularly as a social with friends, possibly on Friday nights or weekends.
We begin to look forward to these social regular events. Our thoughts throughout the week may often draw to the weekend wind-down, the high, the party, forming an alliance or friendship with the substance rather than simply enjoying the company of friends.

 It is like when you make a new friend. That initial contact was pleasurable, and you arrange catch ups, as you begin to trust that person. You enjoy how the friendship makes you feel. You look forward to the time spent together, encouraging one another. These friendships are often healthy and trustworthy relationships.

 Unlike with a substance, the relationship is only one-sided. It begins to steal our thoughts, captivating our desire for more. A friendship or alliance begins to take root, deceiving us into a false sense of joy and satisfaction, a lie that says we cannot relax or have fun without indulging in alcohol, substance or other vices.

Slowly the body loses its natural ability to produce its own dopamine. The chemical takes the place of the natural and cries out for more, and addiction is birthed often before realising there is a problem. A relationship with familiarity and trust is formed, and our desire for more grows from just social activities to consuming or using at home on our own more frequently.
The cost becomes higher, financially, mentally and physically, to the point of causing loss and pain. We are trapped and the very thought of giving up that substance or action comes with a price tag. The cravings from addictions, the desire, the withdrawals and not to mention giving up something that has become a friend, may seem impossible to let go of. How do we escape the reality of mistakes made, at personal cost to ourselves?

It is much easier to continue in the addiction than to have the courage to face it and deal with it.

I don't claim to know everything about addiction, but I have learned much about its nature, how it affects many people and the cost it takes. I have learned through studies, through many volunteer roles and firsthand experiences with family. I have walked alongside of many who through self-discipline, counselling, surrounding themselves with friends, and enrolling in rehabilitation programs, have successfully gained back control of their lives and are living free from harmful behaviours.

I lost a sister who struggled with alcoholism. She was close to my heart. She was beautiful in nature and was loved by many.

My father was also an alcoholic who eventually took his own life. It was as though he were two people, on one hand a drunk, many days at a time, and on the other, he was kind, gentle and loving.

As a young girl I saw the struggles he had. The drinking to forget his past demons, to forget the pain of war, the pain of loss of children, the pain of the torment in his mind.

I saw him as one with chains of addiction tied tightly around him, restricting his ability to choose life freely.

There were days I saw him drunk with happy laughter, which turned to continual crying with deep emotional turmoil. Music played a huge role in his drunken moods, and I quickly learned what frame of mind he was in by the music he played. Coming home from school, I knew how to behave according to the music I heard as I came in – Bach and Beethoven when he was depressed, happy-loud-beer-drinking music when he was in party mode.

When Dad was sober and feeling mentally well, he showed us much love and affection. His actions would often speak of a good father.

When Dad was withdrawing and craving more alcohol, he would become mean and getting a drink meant everything, stopping at nothing to acquire some money from my mum, money that she may have hidden. He never laid hands on my mother or any of us, but he would smash our belongings and furniture in his demands that she gives him more money to purchase alcohol.

Our family life was a roller coaster of his addiction. Dad had never planned to be an alcoholic. He simply had formed a trust relationship that began with how the alcohol made him *feel*, to progressing to a *need* for it. From a 'Friday Arv drink' with the boys from work, to eventually days of drinking binges, addiction destroyed a good man. It left him feeling worthless, empty, depressed, angry and remorseful, with no hope of freedom that eventually caused him to end his own life.

If there is one thing addiction has shown us, is that it can be overcome, it only takes the person experiencing it to want to seek out help. If this is you, I encourage you to reach out to someone or a community group (like Alcoholics Anonymous) or a professional counsellor and get help. The first step is to admit that there is a problem, then to be brave enough to take the next step.

Addiction Poem

Is it a substance you crave to feed your soul,
A body screaming, just to feel whole.
To wake each day, thoughts beckoning your mind.
Nothing quenches a thirst of this kind.

*'How can I break free from this enemy I take,
Crying out for more, my body does ache.
Trapped in this guilt and a life of shame,
Perpetual patterns, remaining the same.*

*A vicious cycle each new day will send,
How can this nightmare ever end?
Consuming my thoughts, my desires, my dreams,
This dead-end life or so it seems.*

*Numbing the shame, the pain, the sorrow,
Surely there is a better way to follow.
If I could just stop – how easy it would be,
To at last live life, addiction-free.*

*Is this possible, or is it an outright lie,
Would it not be easier to simply die?
But then death is final – buried in the ground,
Ending a temporary problem for a solution not found.*

*Thirst – thirsty – this fire to quench,
Sinking deeper into this muddy stench.
Then you tell me a story, of One who would take my hand,
Pulling me up through this deadly quicksand.*

*Can I trust that this is for me,
For my life as before a mirror I see –
The lies, the fight, the guilt and the shame,
For in no other I can lay any blame.*

*The story goes, He traded all this for me,
My judgement He took, that I may be free.
The lashes, the wounds, the death that He took,
All written down in His history book.*

*But is it that simple, I cannot see how,
I need a solution that fixes right now.
One that will finish and be complete,
Removing the burden, taking off the heat.'*

Yes, it starts with a relationship with Him,
The same way with an addiction, you did begin.
First a taste to see that it's good,
Then a journey of trust, you would.

Trusting in how it made you feel,
At first the experience so surreal.
Unlike Jesus who will lead you to peace,
Addiction will overtake till you cannot cease.

Once trust is gained, you search for more,
Of that which you trust, will it restore?
The answer to this only you can know,
Which roads to follow, where do you go?

I say there's a place of solace and still,
Surrender the heart, the emotions, the will.
Believe then, your Creator – He longs for your trust,
Beginning conversations with Him, a must.

Honesty with all and laying your heart bare,
Communicate with Him if only you dare.
Inviting Him into the mess that you've made.
Taking that first step, your burden the trade.

THE WELL OF LOVE AND RELATIONSHIPS

We are all born to stand in relationship with one another, right back since the beginning of time. I believe Adam and Eve were created to walk together in friendship, love and to be helpmates. There is no denying that humans are sexual beings, and we operate as helpmates, as teams, as families and friends to stand together in a world that thrives on these fundamentals of life.

Quite often our relationships are marred by the emotions that lie deep within our soul. We may sabotage these relationships because of mistrust, betrayal and poor self-worth.
There is always the danger of entering into relationships that are destructive and unhealthy.

There are those who may have a constant longing for love causing them to enter relationships, trying to satisfy the deep longing in their heart. They may be starving for affection or attention, constantly needing to be around friends and others, who don't leave themselves any time to be alone, for fear of isolation and emptiness. This behaviour may repel friends, consuming all their time to try and satisfy their longings and insecurities. They demand so much until their friends cannot give any more. Friends are not meant to fill all the voids and gaps that anyone may feel.

Lust
Lust is another issue that may stem from childhood, possibly when something about sexuality in its ideal form was abused, warped or an association with the self or other becomes about gratification rather than connection. That could be a craving, wanting to be loved, to feel special or important or to feel self-worth. That sensual feeling a person might perceive as something good, can be confused with love. Our actions and behaviours match the desire that we perceive as good, causing us to be involved in unhealthy sexual relationships.

These types of relationships cannot last or be sustained over time, as they are often based on the sensual, immediate emotional state of the person.

Sensuality may cause us to dress or act provocatively to attract sexual attention. If these desires and emotions are not dealt with, an unhealthy pattern of seeking love in unfulfilling ways may occur.

We may not necessarily desire to enter a relationship, but the longing for sexual attention and affection could compromise our wisdom and ability to withstand; therefore, causing us to walk in promiscuity.

Friendships
It is healthy to have friends. We may have a few close friends that we hold very dear to our heart; friends that can challenge, comfort and encourage us; friends that stand with us through the seasons of time. They hold no judgement, instead they propel us to be the best version of ourselves. This is healthy and usually a two-way street.

The danger is when we want friends to meet all our needs and rely on them for our complete wellbeing. When friendships become self-seeking, desiring our friends to make us feel good about ourselves all the time is unhealthy. When we desire our friends to dote on us and give us their attention and time, not allowing them room to spend time with others is also unhealthy. Jealousy and insecurity can breed in our hearts and grow if we want our friends to meet our every need.

Surrounding ourselves continually with friends and people to shut out the noise in our head is unproductive to our personal health. The loneliness we feel, the emotions that are scarred, the disappointments, the childhood traumas, and low self-worth need to be acknowledged and recognised, to allow ourselves to heal and grow, otherwise our craving to be built up and emotionally affirmed by friends will never be quenched. We may find we move on from friend to friend, as they no longer satisfy our needs.

Sometimes these friends leave us as they can no longer support a friendship that has become one-sided. The life that sparked the friendship was diminished through destructive demanding behaviours.

Remember, friendships are healthy, and we are created for relationships, and if we weren't, we would never experience loneliness, betrayal, loss and love.

Marriage

I married at sixteen out of a desire to be loved and belong. Not that I wasn't loved by my parents, but my perception of myself and my insecurities grew as a child. There were many issues in my childhood life: a father who was an alcoholic and a mum who did her best to keep the family happy and healthy. To say the least there were many uncertain times, when food was scarce, continually moving house, constant change of schools, Dad's mood swings and feeling the weight of responsibility to behave well to keep peace in the home. There was also the question in my mind constantly playing out as I grew older, concerning my father, whether he was my paternal father or not. My sisters and brothers were all blonde and fair skinned, where I have a darker complexion and dark brown hair. When drunk there were a few occasions when Dad would spill the beans, commenting that he was not my father. This caused insecurity and feelings of rejection to grow deep in my heart. I was uncomfortable with family photos as I felt that I did not belong. My insecurity grew with age, and I longed to have someone in my life, that I thought would make me feel complete and give me a sense of belonging. Later, as a young adult, I learned the truth about my real father, his nationality and the circumstances around my conception.

I could blame Mum for her lack at times and I could blame Dad for his displays of behaviour that implanted fear, insecurity, shame and poor self-worth. The truth is that I am accountable for my actions as an adult. How I choose to move through these deep-seated mindsets is on me. I learned to choose the way of forgiveness, to face the lies of the thoughts implanted in my soul.

This was not a quick remedy and as I had married young, longing for someone to make me feel complete, I had to work through my issues while being married.

Before long, I was a young mum of three children to raise and a husband to love. Yes, you guessed, this was not a bed of roses and came with many challenges and great difficulty. The relationship was not easy as two vastly different people were learning to live together harmoniously. Two very different backgrounds, ideals and expectations. We are now married for over forty years and have grown together as one. We have learned to love, forgive, understand one another and enjoy the fruits of a successful marriage.

In marriage, I have learned to love myself, with the love needed to know how to love others. I learned the truth about forgiveness. I learned to become secure and have complete peace. Later in this book I will reveal how I was able to sustain peace throughout my life, how I learnt to drink from a well that is my source and satisfies my soul.

LOVE AND RELATIONSHIP POEM

Where is my True Love, that I cannot find?
I search and search – it consumes my mind.
A love that will complete, the inferior part of me,
Chasing this love, I hunger relentlessly.

A love that will fill the desires of my heart,
Without this love, my life falls apart.
Consumed with this longing, I search far and wide,
Then settle for less, to have someone by my side.

Unbeknown to me, this love cannot sustain,
As my insecurities and fears quietly remain.
Hidden expectations, something amiss,
This love that I found – certainly no bliss.

Captivating thoughts have me longing for more.
Can I be happy without this love, I am not sure.
One broken love that leads to another,
Endlessly pining for new lovers to discover.

I must drink of many lovers to quench this thirst lying within,
Parched and dry, drinking again and again.
At last, I see hope, as I glean a glimpse of me,
Understanding and recognising insecurities I see.

Finally, I found love, that holds no mystery,
A love for myself, dispelling insecurity.
My thirst no more the unquenchable kind,
The longing, the emptiness that once plagued my mind.

For I have now learned to first love me,
As completeness comes and my heart is set free.

THE WELL OF DEPRESSION, SUICIDE AND SELF-HARM

Depression, suicide and self-harm are very real issues that many of us face. I do not claim to be an expert in this field, but through the many years of my volunteer roles, including coming alongside of others as they work through these issues has given me insight and understanding. Also, my experience with my own family has given me true empathy, compassion and love that I seek to provide. I have walked with many through times of depression, suicidal thoughts and self-harm. It saddens my heart to see many walk this difficult road. I have also experienced the pain of losing ones that I love through suicide.

In my younger years there was a time in my life where I wanted to end it all. The overwhelming sense of hopelessness far outweighs rationality. My thoughts were consumed with the pain and loss of hope that caused me to go into a world of despair and disfunction. This often left me with no desire to rise in the morning, to go outdoors or even eat, finding myself hashing over failures, fears, unworthiness, all perpetually circling round and round in my thoughts.

In my experience, it is very difficult to pull oneself out of those thought patterns. Staying in that well and drinking from the source of where it began made it seem impossible to shift. We may not have any understanding of why we feel the way we do, because there is just darkness and gloom all around. It may be a medical condition that we have no control over, or it may be stemmed from past trauma, maybe from immediate loss, betrayal or disappointment. Regardless of how or when we began our struggle, there is always hope.

Psychiatrists, psychologists and counsellors also hold great value in assisting us as we work through the pain and emotions, as quite often we cannot see where the issues lie nor how to process what we feel. The perspective of a professional can give us the insight we need to navigate through our life's journey. There is also a path of faith in God, that gives us hope for our future. Confiding in a friend or a family member that we trust, may also assist us in working through some of these issues, as knowing that we are supported and valued forges confidence in ourselves. Seeking help is beneficial and fruitful in bringing us to a place of peace and a hope for our future.

Find some good wells to drink from. There are many help agencies in most communities that are geared up to help us see life in a positive way.

Many of these are affordable or made freely available. There are likely to be mental health hubs in your community, where one could spend the day developing friendships and participating in social events, so as not to be alone. We may have to push ourselves to go, withstanding all temptation to stay home and in bed. Many of these hubs run programs and activities that can help us shift our thinking. This can help us out of our thoughts and situation and gain perspective.

A phone conversation with community organisations and agencies geared up to help with specific needs, crisis support, mental health, suicide, addiction, all these can help shift our focus and give direction to our immediate thoughts. The internet easily provides contacts for many of these organisations, with descriptions of their services.

I have had the privilege of volunteering in a mental health hub in my community for five years. The value of these hubs in assisting many through their journey is immeasurable. They work with professionals, volunteers, support workers and more, giving many lives hope, joy and a sense of belonging. They offer life skills, craft, sport, outdoor activities as well as leading others with encouragement and care. A community is formed in these hubs, leaving less room and time to dwell on oneself, spurring one another on to succeed.

Churches are another community hub, that offer an immediate village, they are a great way to connect with other members of your local town or city. For millennia, humans have had churches of faith-based gatherings and places to connect and grow their faith. If you feel like something may be missing from your life, a connection with God and others may be a path worth pursuing.

Focusing on our own challenges can magnify them, so what about shifting your focus to others, taking on the role of caring for the needs of others. Volunteering time in a community group may well assist us in shifting that focus on a tangible, fulfilling way. Most communities have organisations that value volunteers, like Meals on Wheels, Lifeline, Red Cross, nursing homes and so on.

Depression, Suicide and Self-harm Poem

There is a well of depression, suicide and self-harm,
Causing turmoil in the mind, leaving storms to calm.
How do I break free from the torment in my mind,
How do I stop drinking from a well of this kind?

I just want to stay in bed and sleep through the day,
Hoping this misery ends, and all to go away.
If I stay asleep, then I don't have to think,
Possibly my thoughts, disappear and shrink.

The constant fears, the nagging in my head,
This too shall pass or so they said.
Do I muster the courage, to leave this dark well?
Even for a few hours, giving me a spell.

Can I take each day slow, and find a place to be,
One that would stir hope, for my eyes to see.
Will I find a well to drink from, that will lift my head,
Some laughter, some fun, time with friends instead.

To make that difficult choice, to rise in the morn,
To step outside and stretch on the lawn.
To go for a walk and drink of the beauty,
Meditating on this as though watching a movie.

There are community groups, that can help me get through,
The quandary of days when I feel blue.
The choice I need to make, seems difficult to face,
To see my day through in a better headspace

Not to think on tomorrow or the weeks to come,
But to live each day, each moment, one by one.

The well of unforgiveness

Unforgiveness is a difficult topic. It comes with many emotions and runs deep in the heart of a human being, and it can even cause us to become physically sick. Our souls are not meant to carry great turmoil long-term. Hatred breeds out of unforgiveness, then in turn often flows out of our mouths.

There was a period in my life where unforgiveness sneakily became a stronghold in my heart. Unbeknown to me, I would act, think and make choices that came out of unforgiveness. I became self-protecting, self-sufficient, cynical and somewhat cold. My heart had hardened without me realising where it was coming from. Negative thoughts would pop into my mind, constantly wanting to criticise.

Due to naively marrying young, marriage was a difficult journey, and having three young children so early in this scenario was not ideal. Many issues arose, and expectations were often not met. I was very skilled though at masking my feelings to the outside world, which made it more destructive as I tended to ignore situations and just move through life.

I say more destructive because if I didn't deal with the core issues, choices I made may have been sudden, drastic or final decisions. Suicidal thoughts played out in my mind, as well as thoughts of shutting down, ending the marriage, and at times making some decisions just to feel better and escape the reality of dealing with life.

Eventually I had the courage to face these feelings, and I would search my soul to try to pinpoint the core issue. Once I knew the core issue, I had a choice to make, work through the problems, seek some wise counsel, forgive, or not forgive. I chose to forgive, then I had to follow through with my actions. I had to walk and talk in the opposite direction to what my mind was telling me. I made a choice to forgive, but my mind and memory had to catch up. Talking in the opposite meant that when my mind replayed memories that had caused pain and turmoil, my first instinctive reaction would be wanting to speak and react out of that memory. Instead, I chose to hold my tongue, stop and re-purpose my thoughts and remind myself that I had dealt with that situation, I had forgiven, and if I had nothing positive to say, I would keep silent until I was able to shift my thinking. When my thoughts drifted in the wrong direction, I would deliberately choose to think on something good. This was not easy, but with conscious practice life became easier. If my thoughts were unkind, I would choose to act kind, which eventually turned situations around.

There was a time when I had lost respect for a person that I loved, and due to that my thoughts would centre around then rather than now, constantly thinking negative, unkind and even hateful thoughts. Even though I had forgiven, and that person was truly sorry on their part, a pattern had cemented in my mind that seemed to override the restoration that had taken place between us. This is where I had decided I would do kind and thoughtful actions, going against what my thoughts were saying. Eventually this broke the pattern that seemed set in stone, and my thoughts toward that person changed, and love was restored and renewed between us. Through this I have also learned that if I have hurt someone and genuinely told them I was sorry, I needed to give them space and time to work through the process of forgiveness.

Forgiveness does not mean that person is let off the hook. It simply means you release yourself from the prison that person has put you in. You step out of that prison and no longer stay a victim. It does not make what that person did insignificant or unimportant, but it gives you the power to walk free. Another way of looking at it is if you carried a heavy backpack everywhere you go day and night, then remove it and toss it away, you would feel light and free.

If you are struggling with unforgiveness and are ready to deal with it, there is always someone you can talk to, a professional counsellor, a pastor or church leader, perhaps a friend who you trust. I understand that some injustices are great and that it may feel as though you betray yourself if you forgive. Forgiveness is for your benefit, for your freedom, letting go of those things that have weighed you down.

You can do this. Nothing is impossible because we have the power to choose.

Unforgiveness Poem

Thoughts consuming my everyday life,
Constricting my freedom, cutting as a knife.
Penetrating deep into my emotions within,
Replaying in my head time and time again.

Oh, the things that were done – cruel and unfair,
Crippling my actions, into a deep despair.
No freedom to fill the desires of my heart,
Constantly looking back from when it did start.

Occasionally a rainbow to follow my dream,
Only to disintegrate or so it would seem.
Two steps forward I dare to take,
With memories flooding back I now forsake.

From troubles deep, I desire to be free,
Oh well! Never mind I guess this is me.
A stumbling block often with a detour in mind,
As the path leads back to what was unkind.

If I give up that memory, then who am I?
Best to hold on, is that really a lie?
Letting go doesn't mean one is off the hook,
Simply a line cut loose, as a fish in a brook.

Freedom to make way through the streams,
Enabled to navigate all those dreams.
Leaving behind that chapter and all that was done,
The weight lifted off; new life has begun.

The Well of the Past

Our past carries many memories, whether they are ones to savour or ones we try to forget. Some memories hold great value and joy in our lives that often cause us to want to stay there or live back in that time.

Life at times may get a little boring or stagnate. I see life as rolling on in seasons, just like the weather, and we have our winter, summer, spring and autumn.

Winter – is the season of loss and grief, disappointments and heartache. It's a cold season, bitter and unfriendly. A season where we may want to isolate and stay under the covers. One where we avoid company and choose to stay alone, in line with our emotions.

Summer – is hot and sticky, uncomfortable and yet beautiful. I liken summer to the season where I push myself to excel even if it is uncomfortable. The cool of the air conditioning is much more enticing than to go out in the sunshine, the beach, a park or a river though it may be beautiful and peaceful. The sticky humid heat beckons us to stay indoors. Once the choice is made to step outside, we face the hot elements to embrace the beauty.

This is the season where I dare to step out and be challenged, learn new things and break new ground. It may be scary, uncomfortable and unfamiliar, but the reward and risk far outweigh staying put in comfortable surrounds.

Autumn – is the season where the leaves turn brown and fall away. The trees become bare and barren. I liken this season to the dry and unfruitful times in life. The season where we face a crossroad that forces change. Nothing is stimulating, new or exciting anymore. Our rhythm of life has plateaued and seems meaningless, like a tree losing its leaves.

Spring – is the season when new life springs forth. Ideas and plans come into fruition. Weddings and significant events bring hope and expectations, joy and laughter, new life and renewed hope.

The past is part of life's seasons. If the winter stays cold and bitter, no new life could possibly spring forth. No new growth, no flowers blooming, nor new births representing life and hope.

If the season stays brown and everything falls away, there would be nothing left. Barrenness would take hold. Life would remain empty and bare.

Each season propels the next season, preparing us for growth, maturity, clarity and much more, and as we grow in strength and wisdom, we become firmly grounded.

Seasons need to be embraced for what they bring, not in a way that is necessarily exciting or joyful, but to allow ourselves to walk through, facing each day knowing that the season will pass. If we walk through grief, we need not stand alone. We need to know that there is always hope and this season will pass.

I have been through seasons of great grief and loss. The loss of those that have suddenly passed, those who were expected to pass and the grief shared together with family members. Those losses will always remain and will shape the next phases of my life. Do I dare allow myself to move through the emotional turmoil and see beyond the season I am in, or do I continue to drink from this well of pain?

Regret is another season of the past that may be a stumbling block to move forward. Mistakes made, past failures and wrong choices can bring regret. These times are temporary and yet somehow keep us from entering a better season, constantly dwelling on those things, feeling a sense of failure and a belief that the consequences are set in concrete, or believing that 'this is my lot' and things will never change or improve. Some consequences are difficult and must endure a season, but there is always hope. The seasons of consequence and regret can be turned to one with promises of a future that is brighter. Forgiving ourselves is an important part of pressing forward. We need to look for ways to change our situation into something positive. Don't live in the despair but choose to find ways to make the best out of those past situations.

For me, I began by looking at all the great positive things in my life and being thankful. I realised it was hard to see what I have in front of me when I was continually looking back, and so I made a choice to look for ways to develop personal growth, out of those regrets, turning them around to future hope, rather than being consumed with hopelessness. I put positive and encouraging quotes on my fridge and wardrobe, places that I would see often. I spent time helping others, which became very fulfilling and satisfying, shifting the focus off me. I joined community groups, that had positive effects on my life. Self-help books were also a great tool and valuable in giving me purpose, and the imagination to see my life flourish and grow. I had a future, and I decided not to allow my past to dictate my future anymore, I had to stop drinking from the well of pain and regret.

The well of the past can be a destructive one to drink from. It becomes bitter, crippling and lifeless. It is vital to find a well, a source of life that will restore our soul and give us a clear perspective for our future.

The past has a way of keeping us trapped and not allowing us to see beyond that season or situation. Letting go of the past, looking ahead to our future is not necessarily easy, as it involves a deliberate choice we make to focus on the new rather than the old. Consciously making that choice not to look back, not staying in what was.

This does not cancel out the memories, whether they are good, bad, sad or happy. It simply means those memories do not hold us bound, nor do they dictate our future wellbeing. I had to constantly remind myself that they are just memories of past events, imagining myself putting those thoughts into a box and closing the lid. This helped me to separate those memories from my mind, just as you would put away a box of letters. The letters are there but not open for me to read; therefore, they held no sting unless I re-open them and dwell on those events.

I also wrote final visible letters, addressed to those things or people, how I felt, how it affected me, how much it hurt and unfair the situation was, then to scrunch them up and throw them in the rubbish. Sometimes unsaid words held me in unforgiveness and memory, and this action would bring healing to my heart, helping me to let go, process and heal, reminding me to think on the future rather than thoughts that would drag me down from the weight of past events and choices. I would choose to walk and talk in the opposite of what my mind and emotions would say. If my thoughts were negative, I would choose to do something or say something positive, like go for a walk instead of brooding, or react positively or kindly as opposed to an instant harsh reaction, this proved a difficult task as those memories, those events and losses were very real. It felt like I was acting out an ideal despite the emotions I felt. These actions and reactions became realities in my life, diminishing the memories, and forming new patterns that became wholesome habits. Learning to consistently drink from the right wells has been my sustenance, my joy, my source of life. I say learning because even though I knew the wells that I needed to draw from, it is a continual work in progress to steer away from harmful wells.

The past Poem

Is it thoughts of the past occupying my mind,
Stealing my joy, robbing me blind?
Continually looking back is a trap and a snare,
Brooding over events, unjust and unfair.

Regrets of the past, holding me bound,
Immobilising my ability to gain new ground.
Drinking from this well of the old and the past,
Cheating my future of joy unsurpassed.

Thoughts closing in of the failures once felt,
Stifling my ability to push through what life dealt.
Perhaps memories of the good that had once been,
A life visioned with hope and dreams once seen.

Blinding my mind, till the eyes have grown dim,
Glimpses of happiness now looking quite grim.
The past had a way of dictating my future at hand,
Choices were made as disappointment took command.

Laying aside the past seems an impossible task,
A risk to take, I dare to ask.
To allow myself to hope once again,
Putting down those memories filled with disdain.

Choosing a new path, leaving regret on the shelf,
Starting afresh with love and forgiveness of self.

The Well of Pain

As I write this chapter I reflect on my own journey of pain. Two years prior to turning sixty I was diagnosed with polymyalgia rheumatica and rheumatoid arthritis.

This progressed rapidly, and within a couple of months I found myself in excruciating pain. For the first four months I could barely walk, sit or move. Any endeavour to move or simply lift a hand or foot caused pain in every joint and muscle imaginable. Fevers and shivering also came with this chronic disease and I could barely lift the sheet off my body without tremendous pain in my fingers and wrists, as well as the weight of that sheet over my feet causing great discomfort. The swelling in my feet, hands and joints, made them stiff and unable to carry out simple tasks, like holding a pen, wearing shoes, turning around, combing my hair, things I would normally take for granted. I spent these months lying on the sofa with pillows propped behind my shoulders and head to elevate me to a half sitting position, which would somewhat ease some of the discomfort. If I needed to get up, I would painfully move to a sitting position, then count with the goal of getting up on *three*. I knew this would cause the most pain, as with swollen stiff knees and muscles that didn't support me, it took every ounce of courage to get up. Once I was up it felt like my feet were standing and walking on glass. This chapter and season in my life was one that gave me understanding of chronic pain.

I have always been well, and mobility was never an issue. I very rarely took sick, and I was physically fit. Having to go to a doctor was rare. This pain was foreign and scary and something out of my control. I had no idea how or if I would get through that season. Would I become unable to walk, or would I be able to use my hands – these were questions that were often on my mind.

Two years have gone by, and I have improved greatly. I am now stable with the medications I continue to take. The process was slow, with much trial and error on what medications worked best with the least side effects.

I am no stranger to the journey of pain. In a season of pain, we must hold onto hope and not surrender to the mental effects long-term pain can cause. When it comes to dealing with chronic pain, it may help to see life as a process of one day at a time, and when particularly difficult, maybe one hour at a time.

Through my journey, I had to work through learning to manage each day as best I could. I decided that I was not going to drink from a well of self-pity, hopelessness and despair. I would surround myself with wells to drink from that would bring refreshment and distraction.

As I am one who believes in a God who created me, I looked to Him for help. Television would bring solace, and I spent hours watching as I lay on the sofa. Movies were what I was drawn to, especially comedies, as this would bring joy and laughter amidst the pain. They say that laughter is the best medicine. Those moments helped me forget the pain, which gave me reprieve mentally. It was too difficult to read or phone a friend or family member due to the pain of holding something in my hand. Food was another difficult task, as was a visit to the toilet. Meals were dropped in from friends and family, causing me to feel very loved and cared for.

I began meditating on the good things I had. The things that I had seen and enjoyed would shift my thinking in a positive way. I would talk to myself, encouraging myself that I can walk through this and do what I need to do to get through the day. I would sing songs that had hope to encourage my soul, which helped me dismiss fear, anxiety, feelings of being useless, and worrying about my future, not allowing those thoughts to consume me. There were times of struggle, when it seemed impossible to do anything, yet I knew it would take courage and thinking opposite to what the body feels.

Opposite meaning that despite the pain, I would tell myself repeatedly that I can do this, and that it's just another season. Thinking about becoming well, turned into believing that I will be well, no matter what my body felt like. These are the moments that my willpower had to be stronger than my feelings and failing body.

Faith to believe that I would get well played a huge part in my state of mind. I would think about my family, my grandchildren, my husband, this gave me courage to keep on hoping and believing. I played music that had messages of hope and peace as I slept.

I hope that my story will encourage anyone in a similar season to muster the courage to keep on going, to believe for healing and to get well.

Pain Poem

This pain in my body I can no longer bear,
Why is it so – does anybody care?
Movement impossible with pain so unreal,
Intensity increases till I no longer feel –

The joy of life and passion to live,
Drained from my spirit, like a leaking sieve.
How long must I survive, enduring this plight?
My body fast failing, losing the fight.

To hope once more that I may be well
Is this a curse? Am I under a spell?
Have I sinned so great deserving this plot
Is this my life – is this my lot?

Medications and pills just to ease the pain,
Only to see it fail, yet once again.
Where does my help come from? I am in despair,
These questions I raise as I shout, it's unfair.

Whilst many around me, well and happy at best,
I am out of my mind, is this a test?
Enough already, I cannot sustain anymore,
Rather I would die, that is for sure.

Well-meaning souls, come with good advice,
Gritting my teeth, I think *just be nice.*
I feel so alone that I isolate and hide,
With no one to tell – not one to confide.

I must not give in to those thoughts that surround,
One day at a time is best I have found.
Discovering ways to simply find joy,
A task or an activity I must employ.

Helping me through each day that I face,
Those moments of solace I must embrace.
Giving me hope for that healing I seek,
Seeing me through week after week.

The Well of Wealth

Wealth is a positive commodity in one's life, but there is a misconception that wealth will bring happiness and define success. Sure, money could buy all our needs plus all the pleasures our hearts may desire, leaving nothing lacking financially, but wealth cannot sustain one's emotional needs. We may experience short term joy once we purchase that new car, house or boat. Reality hits as the days pass, fading the joy of those new possessions. Their value lessens and they become stale, familiar and less appealing, and often cause a desire for the next new model.

The feelings of pleasure that wealth creates is temporary. Those feelings cannot sustain our wellbeing, our self-worth or our deep desire to be at peace. Those longings can only be satisfied from within.

The thirst for more wealth will not solely satisfy our lives. Danger comes into play for the temptation to gamble, dreaming of those big wins, and longing for that sudden wealth to fix everything. The old proverb says, 'For the love of money is the root of all evil' (1 Timothy 6:10).

Wisdom, and not wealth is the key to success, for wealth without wisdom seems foolish when one doesn't know how to maintain that wealth. King Solomon could ask for anything he wished. He chose wisdom over wealth (1 Kings 3:1-15). Solomon understood the value of wisdom over wealth. It takes wisdom to foresee a good investment, to choose those friends that we will keep close to our hearts, to buy or not to buy. Wisdom will steer us in the right path in making decisions about life, finance, marriage and much more. A wise person will value money but not run after it or be consumed with it, they will save to gain wealth, work hard and wisely invest. If your finances only allowed you to save one dollar per week, you would begin to watch that dollar grow and increase in value. In turn you will foster a lifestyle of saving.

    Growing up in poverty taught me to spend all that I have to the last dollar, even to the point that I would give away what was left as those dollars held no value to me. I was well accustomed to have nothing left each week. If we do not value money or possessions or anything else, we will not take care of it, save, treasure or guard it. We will become frivolous as it holds no worth or value. Money earned through labouring hard holds value as opposed to wealth gained freely or suddenly. Work can keep us from being lazy and give us purpose and meaning.

    There is nothing wrong with being wealthy, it is good, but to chase after it, consuming our thoughts and time may leave us empty, frustrated and dissatisfied.

WEALTH POEM

The wealth of the world enters the heart,
To gain all its worth appears to be smart.
Working, working, working just to gain more,
Oh, to have the newest model car and more.

Pokies, lottery tickets a promise of return,
Longing for that jackpot one day we yearn.
Dreaming dreams of all that riches can buy,
Ending all troubles is simply a lie.

Wealth cannot buy happiness in the heart,
Though it will easily fill that shopping cart.
Money cannot satisfy an emptiness within,
Nor still the mind, from the noise and the din.

Drinking from the well of wealth we may relish,
Dissatisfaction taking hold, all becomes foolish.
Till thoughts are consumed with a desire for more,
Leaving our hearts empty and poor.

The Well of Escape

While social media is a great tool in this present age, it may also be a distraction from facing the realities of life. I had to learn to discern the difference between a short break from worry and fear or an avoidance of facing reality, using social media and television. Sometimes it can be fruitful in order to regain strength to face whatever we might be facing. That short break can shift our thoughts, our mood and our perspective on dealing with situations. When I was sick and watched comedies, it helped shift my thoughts from the pain I was in, proving to be helpful in getting through the day. Then there were the unhealthy times when I continually watched movies, scrolled on Facebook and read novels to escape what was going on in my head. I didn't want to face or deal with situations that held pain, disappointment or other matters of the heart.

Avoiding issues does not do anyone any good. There comes a point when we need to face the realities of life and work through the issues that we face. Counselling may be helpful, friends' perspectives or even self-help books, as others may see through our blind spots and often uncover the truth of the matter. The longer the avoidance, the more difficult it may become. The pain diminishes and the situation loses clarity, making it difficult to discern what the issue is. It becomes one more thing stuffed and hidden in the heart, slowly concealing that there is anything wrong. This may cause bitterness, and the heart may harden with time.

Countless times I would opt to go to the beach or a bushwalk instead of escaping through media or other means. I would choose the secluded area of the beach, where I would sit, journal, talk out loud about all the things that bothered, hurt or disappointed me. Writing became a great way for me to process my thoughts and feelings. I would write down how I felt, or how a situation or person made me feel. I would write about my hopes, dreams and disappointments. Sometimes I would keep what I wrote and other times I would scrunch the paper up and toss it in the bin, as though tossing away the noise in my head. This gave me great clarity and peace.

Sometimes I would just sit for a while quietly on the sand or a nice big rock, just to view the beauty, or I would stand on the shoreline, allowing the cool water to wash my feet, refreshing my mind and stilling my thoughts. Sitting there in the vast beauty of creation, made me feel safe and secure, a knowing that I can whisper, shout, cry out to the heavens and be heard. This refreshed my soul, and I trusted that I would be okay.

If we are struggling with the noise in our head and trying to shut it out through escape, we could try going to a quiet place and working through this. We can take a break from devices and allow our minds and hearts to be still. We can be brave enough to face the realities in our lives and work through them. We each have value and matter more than we could possibly imagine. We all have the potential for growth and strength that will catapult us into our next season of life.

ESCAPE POEM

How do we escape the noise in our head?
Thoughts, emotions and words that were said.
The problems we face as we live on this earth,
Some stemming from childhood, since our birth.

Facebook, Instagram, television and more,
Shutting off our mind, closing the door.
Existence becomes a superficial world,
Pushing aside pain and accusations hurled.

Unreality and ideals compromising our mind,
Escaping our thoughts, leaving us blind.
Till conscience is seared, foregoing daily tasks,
Hiding the emotions behind fanciful masks.

What happens when we shut off the commotion?
Silence begins setting the pace in motion,
To allow ourselves to hear the thoughts once hid,
Opening our mind as we lift that lid.

Finally, to allow the process of thought,
Dealing with life the way that we ought.
Difficult it may be, yet a far greater prize,
Seeing life once more with new visioned eyes.

No longer need to shut out the noise,
As our hearts are now free, and we stand with poise.

The Well of Living Waters

This final chapter concludes with a well of a different kind. It is the well of Living Waters. This is the well that I have learned to drink from for most of my life. This well I have tested and tried, and it has unmeasurably proven to me a source of life that I can trust and be satisfied with.

As a young child I always believed in the existence of God. Mum often sent me, and my sisters, to Sunday School, at the local church in whichever town we lived in at the time. As we sang songs of God's love, I felt something tangible in the way of love and happiness. This real experience is where I first learned to trust and believe in God who loved me. Faith began in my heart and was activated during situations in my home life that would breed insecurity and fear.

When my dad was drunk, loud and smashing things, harming himself in the process, I would hide under my bed and pray. As I hid, a peace and calmness would come over me, reinforcing my belief in God. It didn't change my father, but it changed me.

The impact of a dysfunctional family life left me with many deep issues that over the years I have had to work through. This is where the love for the Well I learned to drink from grew as I developed a relationship of trust between God and me, which became my source of life, a Well. I noticed how I felt after talking to Him, offloading my cares and thoughts. I would feel peace and sense a surrounding of love over me that would move me to tears, not sad but joyful, filling my heart. These moments sustained me, helping me to walk through the issues I faced. Not every situation had the outcome I wanted or thought I needed, but I changed as I spent time drawing from that well. I became stronger inwardly, freer, happier and at peace. I would read the bible and look for verses that would encourage, instruct and help me. Most bibles have a concordance at the back, making it easier to find help for certain situations. If I was afraid, I would look up the word 'fear' in the concordance, and it would show all the verses on fear. The more I read, and talked to Him, putting into practise what I had learned, the more loved and secure I felt.

Over the years I have dealt with many different emotions, some deep-seated and others have come as I live life.

My first taste of this Well of Living Waters was as that young child hiding under her bed, then later again as a young teenager, when I attended a church with my mum. The memory of that one service left an impression of an overwhelming love that encompassed me. I longed for that love, and I didn't know or understand how to sustain it.

In my search to be loved, and to belong, I wanted someone tangible, that I could see and feel, that was mine or so I thought. This led me to marry at the age of sixteen. At seventeen, our first child was born, yet I still felt empty and lost, even though I thought I had all I needed.

It was then that I decided that I would go back to that Well and drink of what held familiar memories and hope. I joined a local church and grew from there. We had two more children and at twenty I had three small children all under three years old. For the past forty-two years I have learned to drink from a well that has been my life source, my joy, my peace, my counsel and my hope.

Many times, the road was tough, and I would become weary, feeling that there just didn't seem to be enough water to sustain me. The Well seemed dry, but it was me who stopped drinking from its source. Those were the times I drank from springs of hurt, disappointment, pain and sorrow. Strongholds of fear, insecurity and emotional turmoil arose from a marriage that was difficult; however, to this day we are still together, at peace and hold a love that has matured into something beautiful.

I want to share a scenario out of the bible that revealed to me this Well that I drink from.

Jacob's well: Jesus, tired from a long walk, sat wearily beside this well. A Samaritan woman also came by to draw water from this well alone. This was an unusual scenario. Perhaps her lifestyle led her to be ashamed and insecure, leading her to choose a time to go to the well when she would be alone. She was well known and was despised, especially by men. She was living in an era of much prejudice, classed as lower standard through birth and yet Jesus spoke to her:

John 4:5-18 (NLT translation)
Eventually he came to the Samaritan village of Sychar, near the field that Jacob gave to his son Joseph. Jacob's well was there, and Jesus, tired from the long walk, sat wearily beside the well at noontime. Soon a Samaritan woman came to draw water, and Jesus said to her, 'Please give me a drink.' He was alone at the time because his disciples had gone into the village to buy some food. The woman was surprised, for Jews refuse to have anything to do with Samaritans.
She said to Jesus, 'You are a Jew, and I am a Samaritan woman, why are you asking me for a drink?'
Jesus replied, 'If you only knew the gift God has for you and who you are speaking to, you would ask me, and I would give you living water.'
'But Sir, you don't have a rope or bucket,' she said. 'And this well is very deep. Where would you get

this living water? And besides, do you think you're greater than our ancestor Jacob, who gave us this well? How can you offer better water than he and his sons and his animals enjoyed?'

Jesus replied, 'Anyone who drinks this water will soon become thirsty again. But those who drink the water I give will never be thirsty again. It becomes a fresh bubbling spring within them, giving them eternal life.'

'Please, Sir,' the woman said, 'give me this water! Then I'll never be thirsty again, and I won't have to come here to get water.'

'Go and get your husband,' Jesus told her.

'I don't have a husband,' the woman replied.

Jesus said, 'You're right! You don't have a husband – for you have had five husbands, and you aren't even married to the man you're living with now. You certainly spoke the truth!'

....
....

John 7:37-39 (NLT translation)

'Let anyone who is thirsty come to me and drink. Whoever believes in me as scripture has said, rivers of living water will flow from within them.'

....
....

These passages are a truth in my life, and I feel those rivers of living water flowing from within me. The more I draw from His well and His Word the more satisfied I become.

You might ask – how might I draw from this well? It begins with a journey of life and a measure of faith. This faith may only be small, but it grows as we exercise our faith and put it into action. I chose to join a local church, to hear the messages and teachings of how to apply the word of God, that is written in the bible, into my life today. It became relevant to my personal circumstances. It changed my thinking, my perspective and gave answers to many problems I faced, and my faith grew as I applied these words to my life and saw results that brought peace and joy to my soul. Sometimes applying the Word is very difficult as it involves putting trust in someone we cannot see and aiming for high ideals like forgiving injustices. This requires faith as we cannot see the outcome or maybe not understand why. Why shouldn't I indulge or do as I please in what seems right in my own eyes?

Many perceive the bible to be just a rule book of 'dos and don'ts', a book of condemnation and consequence. I found that it is a source of life that I can live by. It is a Well to drink from. The 'don'ts' are more about the foreseeable future and the wellbeing of my soul, from One who cares about my heart. He knows what will harm me physically and emotionally. He knows what will bring factions in my mind and confusion to my thoughts, what will destroy me emotionally and leave me empty and bare.

The 'dos' are more about what will cause me to flourish and grow. To be healthy through to my innermost being, rather than just rules to live by 'or else'. It teaches me to guard my heart, for out of it will flow the springs of life (Proverbs 4:23).

There were times I had to seek counsel from others who had wisdom and insight on certain situations. I joined small connect groups where I would learn valuable life lessons. I have made lifelong friends through these groups that accept and love me for who I am, friends who are honest and challenge my thinking, keeping me well-grounded and balanced.

I have also had disappointments and been let down by those around me. After all, we are all humans doing life together. We all have our own insecurities and imperfections.

I have had to face many of life's challenges. Having faith and staying close to the Well does not mean I won't face loss, betrayal, heartache and disappointment. Life happens, and we live in a world that is imperfect. Adam and Eve were imperfect from the very beginning. They were made perfect, but they had a mind and heart and an ability to choose what was right in their own eyes.

Sin entered the world, and shame began when they ate of the fruit which was forbidden. They hid from God as they felt naked and ashamed. Was it a rule or one of those 'don'ts' I previously mentioned to benefit their souls?

I believe it was mankind's very first lesson in the responsibility of having free will. Some will argue and question why we were created to have a will to choose. Why weren't we programmed on auto pilot to simply follow rules?

Choice unlocks the freedom we have to live or to die, to be free or bound, to understand cause and effect and consequences. Not to view life as rules but wisdom and understanding, knowing what is good for our soul and what brings us harm.

Drinking from the Well taught me about relationships. My first and foremost relationship is with Jesus, the source of the Well. I learned to talk to Him, to confide in Him, sharing my deepest secrets. This is how a trust relationship forms and grows.

When we meet someone for the first time, we don't know them or anything about them. We can't possibly trust them with all our secrets and everything we have. That trust requires time as the friendship grows. Spending time together, confiding and sharing our hearts with one another is when we learn to trust that person by their actions and reactions.

It is through my journey of faith that I have seen my prayers answered, although not always in the way I thought they would be. I felt the embrace of His love. I saw the 'dos and the don'ts' work in favour to benefit my life.

I experience daily joy and peace as I am refreshed from sitting in the presence of the One who loves me.

Many times, in my earlier years I would go to quiet secluded places. I would spend hours talking to God, building a trust relationship. Beaches were my favourite places, to go and meet with Him, where there would be no distractions. I would experience His love pour out over me and in me as I sat in those places. Many questions, many tears and emotions would be poured out to Him. Answers didn't come immediately, nor a voice speaking audibly, but a quiet refreshing peace restoring my soul. Sometimes later I would receive a knowing of what I must do or a knowing that all will be okay.

I yearned for those times alone with Him as trust grew and I became freer. Life was hectic with three young children and those intimate times with God sustained me through the busyness. Over the years I didn't feel the need to go to a quiet place because the Well was *in* me, wherever I was. I became so intertwined in relationship with Him that we became as one. Anytime, anyplace, busy or not, He was there. Often, I am caught unawares with an appearance of talking to myself. Truth is I am talking to Him. He never leaves me nor forsakes me. I am the one that may leave for a time.

There were times when my heart left God, for other wells to draw from. My feelings of hatred, disappointment and betrayal were all emotions that I continued to ignore, rather than dealing with. These are the times I would spend all day escaping my thoughts through watching television and spending endless time with friends. I couldn't bring myself to read the bible as deep down I knew the answers were there, but I didn't want to face the issues deep in my heart. I realised that I was mad at God for not answering my prayers the way I thought He should. I had inwardly directed blame toward God, knowing that it wasn't His fault, that situations arise good or bad because we live with imperfection. If I were to shift that blame, it meant I would have to take responsibility for my thoughts and actions, and I didn't really want to do that. I wanted to stay in my pity party. I still went to church, although a little robotically going through the motions with an empty heart. There came a time when I knew I must face the issues in my heart, else I drift further and further away from His love that has been my stability, my joy and peace. Also, how was I to help anyone else if I wasn't willing to help myself.

I knew that God's love for me was endless, timeless and unconditional, and all I needed to do was to talk to Him and surrender my heart's deepest thoughts. I had avoided these issues for so long that I didn't know where to start – I couldn't pinpoint a particular problem or feeling.

Finally, I sat in my lounge and asked Jesus, 'Where do I start? I don't know.'

It was then that I sensed a quiet voice whispering, 'Start with my Word, open it and read aloud a verse, a page, or just a line. It doesn't matter if it doesn't make sense, because when you open the Word, you open your heart toward me, and I will come. I promise if you do this each day, I will fill your soul and heal those emotions in your heart. I will breathe my breath in you, and you will sing again.'

I chose to surrender and do what He asked. I opened the Word in the silence of my home. The moment I opened that bible I began to weep and be overcome with such a presence of love that surrounded me. I realised, God knows the thoughts and struggles within us, and it's only until we tell Him that He can help, for that is when we give Him the permission to come into that situation. His promise was and is trustworthy and true, as my heart was restored back to Him. That experience brought me into a deeper trust with Jesus.

Throughout the years, I learned to forgive, to trust, to wait, to believe. He spoke healing in my heart through all seasons. I have come to understand that God has my best interest in His heart and that He would do nothing to harm me. How I choose to react makes the difference, in empowering me to be in a position to better help others in their journey of life.

I grew to realise that there was good and evil at war on this earth, and if I asked Him to show me how to make the best of a hard situation, He was faithful. This last year I have faced loss in great measure, and I stand, as a living testament to His grace, with peace and steadfastness in my life. He will turn my ashes into beauty, my sorrow into joy, my mourning into dancing over and over again.

Living Waters Poem

Where is this well that many speak about?
How do I find it when I am in doubt?
I hear of a well, satisfying the deepest of needs,
Quenching one's thirst for counterfeit feeds.

This well is twofold, a secret to live,
One to drink of, then one to give.
First to drink, the water of this well,
Then the outflowing for all to tell.

For those who receive from Jesus will thirst no more,
Rivers of living water to quench and restore.
To enquire of him and drink from His Word,
Refreshing the soul, renewing has occurred.

Bubbling up from within, satisfying one's soul,
Emptiness leaves, one starts to feel whole.
Many may be fooled and stop at one drink,
After tasting a drop, 'I'm well,' they think.

Drink from His instruction, His presence, His ways,
Continually satisfying, sustaining your days.
This well I have found, and I share it with you,
In the hope that you drink and see this is true.

Conclusion

The wells investigated in this book have been written with much thought and consideration. There are many wells we can draw from that are either harmful or helpful. This book focused mainly on the secrets of those wells that may bring harm, to explore the causes and effects they may have on us.

The final chapter being one of Living Waters shows us an antidote to all harmful wells.

Reading and meditating on the Word of God are ways to drink from His well. How do we apply it to our lives today? We meditate on and apply His Word that instructs and comforts us in times of need, creates aims for us to strive for that multiply goodness in our lives.

If you are going through difficult times and you are at crossroads where choices must be made, may you find wisdom and courage to do all that you need to do to live well.

www.ingramcontent.com/pod-product-compliance
Lightning Source LLC
Chambersburg PA
CBHW052151070526
44585CB00017B/2069